THE

NATIONAL

QUARTERLY REVIEW,

EDITED BY

EDWARD I. SEARS, LL.D.

Pulchrum est bene facere reipublicæ, etiam bene dicere haud absurdum est.

VOL. XXXIII. NO. FOR JUNE, 1876.

NEW YORK:
EDWARD I. SEARS, EDITOR AND PROPRIETOR.

1876.

CONTENTS OF No. LXV.

THE NATIONAL QUARTERLY REVIEW.

No. LXV.

JUNE, 1876.

---

1. *The first Discovery of America and its early Civilization.* Translated and enlarged from the German of Dr. F. Kruger. By William Wagener. New York. 1863.
2. *Ancient America in Notes on American Archæology.* By John D. Baldwin. New York. 1872.
3. *Fusang, or the Discovery of America by Chinese Buddhist Priests in the Fifth Century.* By C. G. Leland. New York. 1875.
4. *Antiquitates Americanæ, sive Scriptores Septentrionales Rerum, Ante-Columbianarum in America.* Edidit Sociétas Regia, Antiquarionum Septentrionalium in America. Hafniæ. 1837.
5. *The Discovery of America by the Northmen in the Tenth Century.* By Nathan L. Beamish. London. 1841.
6. *The History of Greenland.* By David Crantz. Translated from the High Dutch. London. 1767.

The honor of having first discovered America has been claimed by almost every race, ancient as well as modern. The Phenicians, Egyptians, Carthaginians, Hindus, Chinese, Japanese, Tartars, Hebrews, Greeks, Romans, Scandinavians, Welsh, Scotch and Irish—all have their advocates to plead their cause more or less earnestly. Amid all these conflicting claims there still remains the unexplained fact that our continent has for countless ages been inhabited by nations in a more or less advanced stage of civilization. There is evidence tending to show that centuries before historic Gaul and Britain were known to the enlightened nations of the East, the American continent possessed rich and populous cities. The valleys of the Ohio and the Mississippi were once teeming with an industrious population, and it is there doubtless that we must seek for the once famous Huehue-Tlapalan of the Toltecs.

Nothing could be farther from our present purpose than to attempt an examination of these different claims. Yet, as bearing somewhat upon our subject, it has been thought not altogether irrelevant to give a brief outline of the more important theories adopted.

One historian,* for example, is fully persuaded that the original settlers here were Carthaginians and Jews. The Carthaginians being a commercial people sent their emissaries over the world, among other places to the western hemisphere. This system of emigration proving hurtful to the State, the Carthaginian Senate put a sudden stop to it, and so those who had been left upon this continent were cut off from communication with the mother country, and turned barbarians. As to the native Brazilians, the learned Portuguese declared that the institution of circumcision alone was needed to render their similarity to the Israelites perfect.

The well-known French writer, Charlevoix, is equally convinced that the first arrivals upon our coasts were from Hyrcania and Tartary; an opinion which geographically speaking is certainly most plausible. To corroborate his views he relates the experience of Father Grellon. This was a French missionary, who after performing his ecclesiastical labors in New France, went to China, where he continued to prosecute his missionary work. While in Tartary he met a Huron woman, whom he had known long before in Canada. In answer to the priest's surprised interrogatories, she assured him that she had been taken in war, and conducted from nation to nation until she had reached the place where she then was, so far from her native land. As accumulative evidence upon this point, the chronicler adds the testimony of

* Emanuel de Moræs.

another French Jesuit. The latter while on his way home from China met a Spanish woman, whom he had formerly known in Florida. Like the Huron captive, she had been taken prisoner by the Indians, and given to the inhabitants of a more distant country, and so passing from tribe to tribe, and country to country, through regions extremely cold, having started from Florida, she at last ended her singular journey in Tartary, where she had married and found a home.* These incidents, even if they possessed an atom of credibility, beyond showing a possible knowledge by the aborigines, of a communication between the two continents, prove little or nothing. Yet it is on much more unsubstantial foundations that many of the speculations concerning the early settlement of America are based. Thus the discovery of a few crosses in Mexico was sufficient to put Lord Kingsborough to an incredible amount of pains and labor to prove that St. Thomas must have visited America. Boturini, a Milanese, came to America in 1735, by direction of the Countess Santibañey who claimed to be a descendant of Montezuma. He too was convinced that St. Thomas had been in Mexico,† and it was even earnestly argued that Quetzalcoatl was no other than the doubting disciple.

We must not omit to mention the Dutch historian, Horn, who strenuously advocates the view that the first settlers here were Scythians. Later came the Phenicians and Carthaginians by way of the Atlantic, and the Chinese by way of the Pacific; others perhaps having been driven hither by tempests. This writer is authority for the assertion that the Phenicians in the Tyrian fleet in the service of Solomon, must have crossed the Atlantic, finding the mines of Ophir in the island of Hayti.‡

All these theories, if we except the vagaries of Lord Kingsborough and Boturini, though for the most part the result of sheer speculation, probably contain some germs of truth. It

* Journal d'un Voyage, etc., 85.

† Boturini *Catálogo, Idea,* pp. 43, 50, 52, Cf. Baldwin's *Ancient America,* p. 195.

‡ *Georgi Horni de Originibus Americanis Libri quatuor.*

has, for instance, been strongly urged that the Chinese as early as the fifth century knew of the existence of the American continent.* The part of the country which they are supposed to have visited, possibly Mexico, was called by the melodious name of Fusang; such being the Chinese name for a plant somewhat resembling the American aloe, said to flourish in the region to which they penetrated. According to Chinese traditions, "five priests of the country of Ripin (now known as Bokhara) went to Fusang, and there spread the law of Buddha. They took with them books, holy images, ritual observances, and established habits of monasticism which altered the manners of the inhabitants." † Forty years later, a Chinese monk, named Hœi-Shin, came from Fusang, and narrated the accounts of his travels, which were duly entered in the official records of the celestial empire.

The course of the travels of these monks seems to have been through Asia to Alaska, by way of the Alentian Islands, and down the American coast to California, or Mexico, or wherever the region of Fusang was situated. It will be remembered that this was the era in which the Buddhist religion was at its height, and its propagandists were sent in every direction to spread its doctrines of the Holy Trinity, and of universal love. It would not, therefore, be surprising that these missionaries, led by the enthusiasm of their creed, should have wandered so far in the service of their faith. But whether from the obstinacy of the native Americans, or from other causes, the Buddhist religion seems not to have made any deep impression upon the aborigines. For, with the exception of a few idols unearthed from Mexican ruins, said to bear some resemblance to the image of Buddha, no traces of that religion have as yet been found upon this continent. At all events, it does not seem that the Chinese ever established any settlements here.

However skeptical we may be concerning the narrative of

* See *Fusang*, by C. G. Leland who follows Prof. C. F. Neumann, cf., also De Guignes in *Mémoires de l'Académie des Inscriptions*, Vol. XXVIII, p. 503, and De Paravey's *L'Amérique sous le nom de pays de Fou Sang*.

† Leland's *Fusang*.

Hœi-Shin, it seems not improbable that the Phenicians, or more properly the Tyrians, visited America at a far earlier period. Allusions to voyages by these people are constantly found in ancient writers.

According to Plutarch* there was an island called Ogygia, lying far to the westward of Britain. Three other islands are described as being near this, and at equal distance from each other, somewhere in the tropics, or literally, "very far toward the hot sunset." A vast continent is described as lying beyond the island Ogygia, five thousand stadia, or about five hundred and fifty English miles distant. By the multitude of rivers which washed down mud and slime, the sea was rendered thick and earthy. The continent was said to be inhabited, especially around the bay, which was described as being not smaller than the sea of Azof. The description of Ogygia has led to the supposition that it could be no other than the Island of Cuba; and it is at least significant that the alleged distance of Ogygia from the continent corresponds exactly with that of Cuba from the mouth of the Mississippi, whose delta is composed of such a mass of slime and mud as seemingly to identify the spot referred to by Plutarch. The bay, not smaller than the Sea of Azof, is of course believed to be the Gulf of Mexico, and the three islands equi-distant are Jamaica, Hayti, and Porto Rico, which are in fact about equally distant from each other.

Another famous Greek historian, Diodorus Siculus,† mentions an island several days' voyage distant from Africa, possessing a fertile soil, mountains and beautiful plains, abounding in navigable rivers, gardens and farms, adorned with magnificent buildings; a description, as Prof. Kruger justly remarks, which cannot be applied to any of the Canaries or Azores, and which corresponds with Plutarch's description of Ogygia. Its discovery is related by Diodorus thus:—The Phenicians had made many voyages of discovery, had ventured beyond the Pillars of Hercules, and had established colonies on the coast of Africa. While exploring the African coast a

* *De Facie in Orbe Lunae*, 26.

† Book v., 19 and 20.

Phenician vessel was driven by heavy winds far out into the ocean. Tossed about for many days by storms, it was at last carried far to the westward, to this island. The crew explored the island, and carried home an account of it. The historian proceeds:—"But when the sea-mighty Tyrians were going to send thither a colony, the Carthaginians prevented them, partly out of fear that many would emigrate thither from Carthage—partly in order to keep an asylum in case of some misfortune occurring. In that event they wished to accomplish a universal emigration to that island."*

There is nothing improbable in this enforced discovery of the western continent. The Phenicians, or Tyrians, were at that time the monarchs of the sea. They were bold navigators, undaunted by any perils of the deep. Their discoveries extended over the whole of the known world, and we may place what has been called the "first discovery of America," as early as somewhere between the eleventh and seventh centuries before Christ.

But far from forming any settlements here, the Tyrians even at that remote date found busy cities already existing; towns "adorned with stately buildings and banqueting houses, pleasantly situated in their gardens and orchards." The remnants and traditions upon this continent of a long extinct civilization, would seem to preclude the notion that the Greek descriptions were drawn purely from the imagination.

There is, of course, no direct evidence that the island mentioned by Diodorus is the Ogygia of Plutarch. It is possible that it may be identical with the mysterious isle of Atlantis, that remote western land, the story of whose marvellous disappearance was so faithfully preserved by the priests of Egypt. The account preserved in Plato's Timaeus is to the effect that there once existed a large western island, with a continent beyond it. On this island, called Atlantis, there existed a great and powerful empire, holding in its sway many of the adjoining islands, and part of the continent. Extending its conquests eastward, this formidable power subdued

* See Kruger's "*First Discovery of America.*"

Africa as far as Egypt, and Europe as far as Etruria; attempted to enslave Egypt, and invaded Greece itself as far as the site of the future city of Athens. Its conquests here met with a sudden check, and its designs of universal dominion were frustrated. The island disappeared beneath the ocean, leaving in its place shoals which rendered navigation in the neighborhood impossible. This, according to Plato,* is the account narrated by the Egyptian priests to Solon. It is an interesting fact that among the few of the ancient records of Central America which have been preserved, there is said to be a similar account of the engulfing of an eastern land, a few of whose inhabitants escaped by boats.† These two narratives, written thousands of miles apart, without the possibility of communication between their authors, would seem to indicate, even to the most skeptical minds, that the story of Atlantis is something more than a mere fable. Brasseur de Bourbourg has gone so far as to attempt to develop a theory that the ancient American civilization was introduced by those inhabitants of Atlantis who escaped the cataclysm, and were carried by their boats to the continent—a theory which has the questionable recommendation of being more easily ridiculed than either refuted or sustained.

In the work entitled "*De mirabilibus Ausculationibus Liber*," by some attributed to Aristotle, we find mention made of the discovery by the Carthaginians of a large island, several days' voyage west from the Pillars of Hercules. The island was rich in vegetation, abounding in woods and navigable rivers. This statement derives its chief importance from the fact of its corroborating to a certain extent the narrative of Diodorus.

Any attempts to explain American antiquities by reference to emigrations from the old world, have proved in a greater or less degree unsatisfactory. The oldest traditions that we have of supposed American discoveries, contain allusions to nations already existing here, and that fact seems to give appreciable weight to the theory that the ancient American races were

---

* Timaeus, vi. † Brasseur de Bourbourg, *Quatre Lettres sur le Mexique*.

autochthonous. According to Professor Orton,* "Geology and archæology are combining to prove that Sorato and Chimborazo have looked down upon a civilization far more ancient than that of the Incas, and perhaps coeval with the flint flakes of Cornwall and the shell mounds of Denmark," so that the belief that all the ancient civilizations upon this continent, including that of the Mound-builders is traceable to South America, seems at any rate well founded.† In the meantime, however, it is as well not to ignore the so-called "accidental theory," of the earliest discovery of America. Observation has shown that as many as fifteen Japanese junks have been storm-driven on our coasts within a not very extended period, and it is quite possible that similar calamities may have befallen luckless voyagers in pre-historic times.

These ancient races, whether native or transplanted have long since passed away, leaving only such traces as the most ancient ruins of Mexico and Central America, which had become subjects of mystery to the inhabitants long before the conquests, or such vestiges as those remarkable mounds scattered over the face of our country from Virginia to Nebraska, and from the Gulf of Mexico to the shores of the great lakes. The mechanical skill and ingenuity displayed in the construction of these mounds are such as could be developed only by an advanced stage of civilization, and geological observations prove that their years are to be counted by thousands. The construction of many of these mounds was perhaps coeval with that of Solomon's Temple. Yet the works of the uncivilized Mound-builders have endured centuries and even millenniums after the temple of the inspired king had crumbled into dust. The subject of the age of these mounds has already been fully discussed in these pages.‡

It is unnecessary to do more here than allude to the proficiency of this strange people in the manufacture of cloth, pottery and domestic utensils; their skill in mining, as shown

---

* *The Andes and the Amazon.*"

† See Baldwin's *Ancient America*, p. 272.

‡ "*Extinct Races of America—the Mound-builders.*" National Quarterly Review, No. XLVII, Dec. 1871.

by the remains of their works on the shores of Lake Superior; or their knowledge of astronomy, as evidenced by their use of telescopic tubes. "In further evidence of their commercial energy, we have copper and silver from the great lakes, pearls and shells from the gulf, mica from the Alleghanies, and obsidian from the volcanic ranges of Mexico."* Their history is still shrouded in darkness. Like the Romans of old, these nations were perhaps over-run by barbarians from the north, and wandered away to the southward,† or were subdued and exterminated, and so the Mound-builders vanished from the earth. If in the gradual solution of the mystery enveloping the origin of this people, the results of historical research coincide with those of rational conjecture, we may yet be compelled to believe the first discoveries of North America to have come from the south.

The mistaken zeal which led the early discoverers of Mexico to destroy all the accessible records, has prevented our obtaining more than a few vague and unsatisfactory traditions that prevailed among the natives. There was a tradition current among both the Mexicans and Peruvians, that the Pacific coasts in those countries had in former times been visited by foreign people who came in ships. It is now pretty generally understood that the empire of the ancient Malays, whose history reached back to the remotest times, once extended over a great part of the Pacific. So extended were their possessions, that it is said the swiftest vessel could not have sailed round the empire in two years. It was probably the subjects of this ocean empire that once traded with the Mexicans and Peruvians. It is well known that the ruins discovered in the Pacific islands bear a startling resemblance to those of Mexico and Central America. Yet if the Malays came to this continent at all, it was as visitors and not as civilizers.‡ After all that has been written and said on the subject, it is still true that the architecture, language, style of writing and general mode of life, of the aborigines of Mexico and Central America differed too

* *Extinct Races of America.*

† Squier's Smithsonian Contributions, vol. I., p. 44.

‡ Baldwin's *Ancient America*, p. 170; and appendix.

essentially from those of any known race, ancient or modern, to justify us in attempting to identify them with any particular one.

Sahagan, the Spanish historian, who is said to have lived sixty years among the aborigines, and written only fifteen years after the conquest, relates "on the authority of Montezuma, who gave the tradition as from the remotest times—it was also proved by historical paintings—that their ancestors as a colony, first touched at Florida, then crossed or coasted the Gulf of Mexico and Yucatan, and finally landed and settled somewhere on the shores of the Bay of Honduras." * Mr. Jones is at great pains to have us believe that the Tyrians after being driven from their capital by Alexander, B. C. 332, fled to the Fortunate Islands and thence to Central America, † however we must confess that we are not convinced by the evidence he adduces to support his views.

But we have dwelt sufficiently long upon what we may call the pre-historic discoveries of America. The mystery and obscurity which invest the subject render it doubly attractive; but we must abandon it, and pass over in silence the early myths and legends of the Peruvians, the Aztecs and the Toltecs, or of any of those other races whose domains, according to Hubert H. Bancroft, before the advent of the Europeans, "counted its aborigines by millions, ranked among its people every phase of primitive humanity, from the reptile-eating cave-dweller of the Great Basin, to the Aztec and Maya-Quiché civilization of the southern table-land,—a civilization, if we credit Dr. Draper, that might have instructed Europe; a culture wantonly crushed by Spain, who thus destroyed races more civilized than herself.‡ Without further comment on these we come down to historic times, when we have distinct evidence of the landing of Europeans on our shores.

It was for a long time felt to be such an imputation on the fame of the Genoese navigator to concede that any European

* See Jones' *History of Ancient America*, London, 1843; also, Kruger's *First Discovery of America*, p. 114.

† *Hist. Anc. America*, pp. 168–172.

‡ *Native Races of the Pacific Coast*, vol. I., p. 10.

had ever visited America before 1492, that the claims of other voyagers have been greatly under-estimated. Even at this late day, in spite of what appear incontestable facts, the claims of the Northmen are far from receiving the universal recognition to which they are entitled. It is of the adventures of these people in the western hemisphere during the middle ages that we wish now especially to speak.

Whether or not Iceland was the *ultima Thule* of the ancients, it is impossible to say. Though the island may have been visited by the Irish at a very early period, * its existence was for a long time forgotten. During the ninth century however, it was visited by a swede named Garder, † and about the same time or a little later, by a Norwegian named Naddok or Nadod, who came upon it quite by accident, when intending a voyage to the Faroe Islands. For the same reason, doubtless, that it enjoys its present appellation, it was called by its discoverer, Snæland or Snowland. Returning to Norway, Naddok informed his countrymen of his discovery, whereupon a Norwegian pirate, named Flokko, or Floki Rafu, determined to go in quest of the island.

After sailing many days, having of course no compass, this pagan pirate, who had probably never heard or read a word of the Sacred Scriptures, adopted the stratagem devised many centuries before by a mariner in a somewhat similar predicament, and sent forth from his vessel a raven which, true to its instincts, flew toward the nearest lands. Flokko steered after the bird, followed it, and so reached Iceland.

Upon his return to Norway, Flokko gave most lugubrious accounts of the newly discovered land. He declared that it was cursed by gods and men; that it was inhabited by a terrible race of giants, who dwelt in caves and in mountains, and who were engaged in "an eternity of strife, in the midst of liquid fire, boiling water and burning stones." ‡ This uninviting picture had the effect for a period of deterring others from visiting the Island. But after Flokko's death, when Norway

* Samlede Afhaudlinger, Bk. I., p. 165.

† Gronland's Historiske Mindesmaerker, vol. I., pp. 92–97.

‡ Otte's *Scandinavian History*, p. 73.

was groaning under the iron rule of Harold Haarfager, it seemed to the liberty-loving Northmen that any land would be preferable to Scandinavia. Accordingly, the Norse Jarl or Earl, Ingolf, fleeing with his retainers from the tyranny of his sovereign, emigrated to Iceland. In obedience to a national custom, Ingolf carried with him the consecrated door-posts of his house. When near Iceland he threw these overboard, and vowed his home should be where these were washed ashore. After drifting for three years, the posts were at last washed ashore, on the western side of the island near the modern town of Reikjabik.* Ingolf colonized and cultivated the island, establishing a republic there somewhere about the year 874. Many of the most intelligent and wealthy of the Norwegian population emigrated thither to escape from the severe laws and enforced religion at home. In the mild and liberal character of its laws and in the general intelligence of its inhabitants, Iceland had now become far superior to the mother country. It may perhaps be gratifying to our national pride to reflect that the Iceland settlements were for the most part on the western side of the island, so that it was within the limits of the western hemisphere that an asylum was thus early offered to the persecuted of Europe; and it would be as well to remember amid the prevalent spirit of the time, that we have already passed through not the centennial, but the milennial of the establishment of republicism in the new world.

The discovery of Greenland followed naturally upon that of Iceland. But there is a sad discrepancy as to dates. There is a long account purporting to be Greenlandish annals in verse, by the Danish poet Christophersen, which puts the discovery of Greenland as far back as A. D. 770. Certain Armenians were first driven thither by a storm, and from Greenland they peopled Norway and America. "But this author writes many things that are not just or congruous, and we must make him allowances as a poet." † If it be true that Pope Gregory IV in 835, by a Bull, committeed in express terms the conversion of Icelanders and Greenlanders to Ansgarins, the "Northern

* Otte's *Scand. Hist.*, p. 74.

† Crantz's *History of Greenland*, vol. I., p. 247.

Apostile," we may conclude that Greenland must have been discovered about 830 by Norwegians or Icelanders.*

The *Iceland Chronicle*, our only other, but far more trustworthy source of information, published about the year 1215, puts the discovery of Greenland as late as 983. At any rate, it seems certain that its existence was unknown, when it was discovered in the latter year by Eric the Red. Eric had been out-lawed in Norway and condemned to a three years exile from Iceland. He had heard of the Rocks of Gunnibroin in the western ocean, and he resolved to seek them. Sailing off with his crew, he discovered a country which he determined to colonize. He returned to Iceland, and for the sake of alluring others to settle in the new country, gave it the false designation of Greenland. In the year 985, "fifteen winters before the christian religion was established in Iceland," Greenland was colonized by settlers from Norway and Iceland.

Shortly after this an Iceland sailor whose name is variously spelt Bjarni, Biorn and Biron, on his return from Norway, learning that his father had gone to Greenland, determined to follow him thither. He met with severe storms, which drove him far to the southwest, where after many days he found himself in the neighborhood of a flat, woody country, and what is now supposed to have been somewhere on the New England coast. Knowing that this could not be Greenland, after the storm was over, Biarni sailed to the northeastward, passing Nova Scotia on the second day, Newfoundland on the fifth, reaching Greenland on the ninth day after leaving New England. Biarni told the Greenlanders of what he had seen, but had nothing especial to relate concerning his discoveries, "and this," according to the Saga, "became somewhat a reproach to him."†

Eric, the Red, though now an old man, determined to go in quest of this new land to the southwest. A fall from his horse, which he regarded as an ill omen, prevented his departure. His son, Leif, however, was a "great and strong man,

* Ib. p. 244.

† Beamish's *Discovery of America*, p. 59.

grave and well favored, therewith sensible and moderate in all things." Leif determined to follow out the expedition himself, and taking Biarni as his pilot, about the year 999 set sail for this unknown land.

Holding their course to the southwestward, these bold navigators were at last rewarded by sight of land. To this they gave the descriptive name of Helluland, or rocky country. Passing beyond this they afterward approached land with level shore, a white sandy beach, where there were no rocks, but plenty of woods, and so they called it Markland, or woody country, being probably Nova Scotia. Two days later they saw more land, and an island near the northern coast of it. Here upon what is supposed to have been the same as the present island of Nantucket, they landed. Re-embarking, they sailed westward, afterward entering a river. Their course, according to the best authority,* seems to have been through Nantucket Bay, beyond the southwest extremity of Cape Cod, thence across Buzzard's Bay to Seaconnet Passage, up the Pocasset River to Mount Hope Bay.

The banks of the river were covered with bushes brilliant with the clusters of berries. Fish, particularly salmon, were seen in great numbers. The soil was rich and to the Norse sailors the air seemed especially mild and genial; while the forests glowing in all the brilliancy of an American autumn afforded a spectacle which to the astonished Europeans must have been the crowning beauty of all the strange scenes. Upon the shores of Mount Hope Bay they built their huts, and prepared to spend the winter.

They called the place in honor of their leader, Leifsbuthir. While here a member of the crew having wandered away from the rest, discovered some wild grapes growing. They spent the winter there, and "Leif gave a name to the land after its sort and called it Vinland it Goda, or the good Vineland." In the spring they returned to Greenland with a cargo of lumber.

On their homeward voyage they rescued fifteen men whom

* Beamish's *Discovery of America by the Northmen*, p. 63.

they found wrecked on a rock; from which circumstance as well as from the fact that he had been the means of introducing christianity into Greenland—their leader was afterwards known as "Leif, the Lucky." "But," says the Heimskringla,* "Eric, his father, said that these two things went one against the other, inasmuch as Lief had saved the crew of the ship, but brought evil men to Greenland, namely, the priests."

A regular means of communication was now established between Greenland and Vinland, and many voyages were made. In 1002, Thorwald, a brother of Leif, led his Norse followers upon one of their expeditions to Vinland. They first went to Leifsbuthir where they spent the winter. In the spring and summer they continued their explorations, but saw no sign of any human beings.† The second winter they also spent at Leifsbüthir. In the next summer they seem to have explored the coast of Massachusetts. They had doubled Kialarness Cape, supposed to be Cape Cod, and were coasting in the neighborhood of Boston Harbor. "This is a beautiful spot and here I should like to fix my dwelling!" exclaimed Thorwald, a wish that met with an unexpected fulfillment. Three boats were drawn up and inverted on the shore and there were three men under each boat. They were the first natives seen by the Northmen in Vinland, and from their diminutive size were contemptuously called Shrællings,‡ chips, that is dwarfs. In the business-like narrative of the Saga, the explorers "caught them all except one, who got away with his boat. They killed the other eight, and then went back to the cape." § We are assured a few lines further on, without any intentional sarcasm, that "Greenland was then christianized."

The natives who had been aroused by the fugitive, Shrælling, rushed upon the shore in great numbers but met with a severe repulse. The Northmen, however, paid dearly for their cruelty in the loss of Thorwald, their chief, who alone of the number was slain.

After the massacre of the Shrællings, more amicable rela-

* *Antiquitates Americanæ*, p. 191.

† *Antiq. Amer.* p. 41.

‡ *Antiquitates Americanæ*, p. 45.

§ Beamish's translation, p. 72.

tions were established, the Northmen continuing to colonize Vinland. On one occasion, Thorstein, another brother of Leif's, started for the new colony, intending to obtain the body of the luckless Thorwald. He never reached Vinland, being storm-driven on the western coast of Greenland, where an epidemic broke out among his crew.

He was hospitably received by one of the inhabitants, whose wife Grimhild caught the contagion and died. Her husband "went after a plank to lay the body upon," when an interesting phenomenon was presented—Grimhild, though dead, "pushed herself up on her elbows and stretched her feet out of bed, and felt for her shoes. At that moment came in the husband, and Grimhild then lay down and every beam in the room creaked." They made a coffin for her, and although her husband "was a large and powerful man, it took all his strength to bring it out of the place. Now the sickness attacked Thorstein Ericson, and he died, which his wife, Gudrid, took much to heart."

An eminent citizen of Iceland, named Thorfinn Karlsefne, who derived his ancestry from the nobility of five nations, soon after Thorstein's death, came to Greenland and sought and won the hand of Gudrid, receiving with her Thorstein's right to Vinland. Gudrid accompanied her husband on a voyage of discovery to Vinland. The fleet consisted of three ships, with a hundred and sixty men, besides cattle for the colony. The history of this voyage is preserved in the "Saga of Thorfinn Karlsefne."

They sailed from Greenland in the year 1007, passed Markland, or Nova Scotia, and arrived at Cape Cod. Continuing southward they beheld the long waste and sandy beach which, whether from the wonderfully white sand, or from the mirage and optical illusions common to Cape Cod, they called Furdurstrand, or Wonder-strand.* They afterward sailed past the island discovered by Leif, where it is said the ducks' eggs were so thick that men could not walk without stepping on them!

In the summer the fishing declined, and with the summer

* *Antiq. Amer.*, 427.

coming on, the colony was altogether in a bad way. Thorhall, the huntsman, commander of one of the three ships, suddenly disappeared. After three days he was found on top of a rock. In the words of the Saga, "They asked him why he had gone there; he said it was no business of theirs; they bade him come home with them, and he did so. Soon after there came a whale, and they went thither and cut it up, and no one knew what sort of a whale it was; and when the cook dressed it, then ate they, and all became ill in consequence." * All these evils Thorhall attributed to the anger of the god Thor, whose worship they had forsaken for Christianity, and an immediate return was vainly urged to the religion of their fathers. "But when they came to know this they cast the whole whale into the sea, and resigned their care to God."

The leaders determined to separate, Thorhall to go northward, with nine men, to explore Vinland, while Thorfinn resolved to go southward. As they were about to depart, Thorhall, the huntsman, gave vent to his feelings in this little burst of song:†

"People told me when I came
Hither all would be so fine;
The good Vinland known to fame,
Rich in fruits and choicest wine;
Now the water pail they send;
To the fountain I must bend,
Nor from out this land divine
Have I quaffed one drop of wine."

And when they were ready and hoisted sail, then chanted Thorhall:

"Let our trusty band
Haste to Fatherland;
Let our vessels brave
Plough the angry wave,
While those few who love
Vinland here may rove,
Or, with idle toil
Fetid whales may boil,
Here on Furdurstrand
Far from Fatherland."

† All these verses bear the stamp of the tenth and eleventh centuries.—*Antiq. Amer.*, p. 144, *note a.*

* Beamish's *Discovery of America*, p. 91.

Our bard was unfortunate, however, and he and his crew were driven by storm across the ocean, to Ireland, "and were there beaten, and made slaves, according to what the merchants have said."

Thorfinn and his followers spent the winter at the head of Mount Hope Bay; Ho'p they called it, and the Indians called it Haup. They landed the live-stock they had brought with them, and here Gudrid gave birth to a son, from whom was descended, among other notabilities, Thorwalsden, the sculptor.

One morning it is said the Northmen saw "a speck," which upon nearer approach proved to be a *Uniped.* After killing one of their number, the Uniped ran away to the northward. They pursued him, till "he ran out into a bay." Then turned they back, and a man chanted these verses:*

"The people chased
A Uniped
Down to the beach;
But lo, he ran
Straight o'er the sea—
Hear thou, Thorfinn."

The appearance of this apparently one-footed creature is explained by the fact that some of the natives are said to have worn a triangular sort of garment, hanging down so low, before and behind, as to cover the feet.

Thorfinn seems to have explored the country as far south as the Carolinas. After an absence of three years, he returned to Greenland, and gave such glowing accounts of Vinland, its richness, beauty and fertility, that many desired to see it. He went back to Iceland, where he built a magnificent house, where he remained till his death. His widow Gudrid made a pilgrimage to Rome, after which she passed the rest of her days in a nunnery in Iceland, founded by her son Snorre.

The Norse people have ever been distinguished for their respect for womanhood. But Freydis, the daughter of Eric, seems to have gone beyond any established limit. She accompanied Thorfinn on his three years' journey to Vinland, and

* Beamish, p. 102.

on one occasion when the Northmen were attacked by the natives, she took a leading part in the battle. Seeing her countrymen waver under an attack by the natives, she seized a sword, and placing herself at the head of the ranks, led her comrades on to victory. She seems not to have been of a loveable nature however. Later she appears to have gone to Vinland with two brothers, Helgi and Finnebogi. She proved generally obnoxious and stirred up disputes in the colony. She procured the destruction of the two brothers and all their followers, slaying the women with her own hand. Extorting a vow of secrecy from her crew, she returned with the ships in triumph back to Greenland. It was pretended that her victims had chosen to remain in Vinland. But the truth afterwards became known, though no severe punishment seems to have been inflicted upon Freydis.

Our chief sources of information on this subject of Vinland's history are the Sagas of Eric the Red and Thorfinn Karlsefne. Another, the Eyrbiggia Saga contains the account of an Icelander named Gudleif, who was driven by storms to the south and west till he reached a land where the people were very savage, and had dark skins. Among the natives was a chief, distinguished from his comrades by his light hair. Recognizing the nationality of the captives, he addressed them in their native tongue. He saved their lives, but advised them to hasten their flight, as their captors are very cruel. He refused to give his name, but asked about a certain Icelander named Snorre Gode, and his sister Thurida. On his return to Iceland, Gudleif related his adventures, and it was supposed that the mysterious stranger was a famous Shald, named Biorn, who had conceived for Thurida, already the wife of another, an affection rather more ardent than the conventionalisms of civilized life would sanction. He had accordingly left Iceland more than thirty years before, and gone to Huitramannaland or White-man's Land, as the region south of Vinland was called, and had not been heard of since. This sensational tale, the subject of an unnecessarily long sort of epic, is the last authentic tidings of the Norse discoveries here; though we are told that in the year 1059, an Irish or Saxton priest named John, "went to preach to the colonists in Vinland, where he was murdered by the heathen." In 1121 * Eric, the bishop of Greenland, went to Vinland for the purpose of reclaiming such of his countrymen as had sunk into the barbarism of the native Shraellings. He never returned, and it is not known that he was ever seen again, though we shall have occasion to allude to him hereafter. In the year 1285 some priests discovered land west of Iceland, supposed to have been Newfoundland; which several years later, by command of King Eric the priest-hater, was visited by one Landa Rolf. †

And here, so far as our own country may be concerned, we leave our Norse invaders. They have left little or no trace of themselves in the shape of ruins or vestiges of any kind. For though the inscriptions on the Deighton Rock are by some enthusiasts supposed to record in Icelandic the fact that the Thorfinn took possession of the country in the early part of the eleventh century, yet others with equal confidence have ascribed those hieroglyphics to the ancient Phenicians. Even the Newport tower, after all the erudition expended upon it, turns out to be of ummistakeable English origin. Still the Icelandic records seem to prove beyond a doubt that at the darkest period of the Middle Ages, at a time when the old world was led by the wild fanaticism of the crusades, the western continent was being explored by the northern Sea-kings, and the long slumbering solitudes of the American forests were being roused by the rude music of

> "Such lays as Zetland's Scald has sung
> His gray and naked isles among,
> Or muttered low at midnight hour
> Round Odin's mossy stone of power."

The minute geographical descriptions given in the sagas clearly indicate the localities as stated above to be correct. But these views are strengthened by other circumstances. Thus, though the description of the relative position of the island to the mainland unmistakeably applies to Nantucket, yet

---

* *Antiq. Amer.*, p. 256. † Ib. p. 40.

in addition to this, we have the statement that the Northmen tasted the dew upon the grass there and found it sweet; this was undoubtedly the honey-dew known to be found on that island. The length of the shortest day is given as from half-past seven to half-past four, which is also true of that neighborhood. But as this subject has already been discussed in these pages * it is unnecessary to add anything more here.

Though the settlement of Vinland was abandoned, the Northmen continued to colonize Greenland for several centuries, and seem to have sent occasional expeditions to the continent. Thus mention is made of a voyage from Greenland to Markland in 1347.† And it is known that they made a number of voyages in the Arctic regions. A stone with Runic inscriptions was found upon the island Kingitorsoak, showing the discoveries by the Northmen in that neighborhood.‡ Runic stones have also been found at Igalikko and Ikigeit, with inscriptions relating to the voyages of the Northmen.

In 1350, the plague called the black death which wrought such devastation in Europe, casting its blight not only on man and beast, but on the soil itself, causing the very trees to wither and die, spared not ill-fated Greenland.§ Many of its inhabitants were swept away, and the natives, who probably owed the colonists no gratitude, turned upon the feeble remnant, well nigh destroying them utterly. After the subsidence of the plague, an attempt was made in Norway to revive the trade with Greenland. But Queen Margaret, "the Semiramis of the north," in 1389 brought a law-suit against the merchants for attempting to carry on the trade without a grant from her, Greenland being claimed as belonging to the royal domain. ‖ At last domestic troubles so much absorbed the attention of the Scandinavians, so many vessels were lost, and so little advantage now resulted from the western colony, which once boasted of its two hundred and eighty settlements, that it was by degrees abandoned; so that when

* See National Quarterly Review, No. LV, for December, 1873, Art. 4.

† *Antiq. Amer.* p. 40.

‡ *Antiq. Amer.* p. 354.

§ Crantz *History of Greenland*, vol. I., p. 263.

‖ Ib., p. 264.

America was re-discovered in 1492, the former colony was known to the Norwegians themselves only by the name of "Lost Greenland."

Casual reference has already been made to Huitramannaland or White-man's Land. It seems to have been known by name, at least, to the Icelanders for many years, and was called Irland it Mikla, or Great Ireland. It is mentioned in the Saga of Thorfinn Karlsefne, and it is said the people "wore white dresses, used iron implements, and had poles borne before them, on which were fastened lappets, and who shouted with a loud voice." * In the Landnámabók or national record of Iceland we find the following: "Ulf, the squinter, son of Högna, the white, took all Reikjaness, between Thokkafiord, and Hafrafell, he married Björg, daughter to Eyoind, the eastman, sister to Helge, the lean; their son was Atli, the red, who married Thorbiörg, sister to Steinoff, the humble; their son was Mar of Hólum, who married Thorkatla, daughter of Hergil Neprass; their son was Ari; he was driven by tempest to White-man's Land, which some call Great Ireland; it lies to the west in the sea, near to Vinland, the good." † From this lucid description we infer that Great Ireland was not far from Vinland. It probably embraced the whole of the eastern limits of the present United States, south of Chesapeake Bay, with perhaps its chief settlement in Florida, between which and Ireland there seems at one time to have been a regular communication. "There existed there (in Florida) a bishopric which had sent teeth of river-horses (hippopotami) as tribute to Rome." ‡ According to the account preserved by Rafn, the Limerick trader, Are Marson, in the year 983, was driven to the shores of Great Ireland by storms. He was there baptised and being held in high esteem was not allowed to return to Ireland. § It is supposed that it was discovered by the Irish, long before the Northmen colonized Vinland. The verdure and fertility of the newly discovered land suggested to the Irish exiles the

* *Antiquitates Americanæ*, p. 37.

† Ibid., p. 210.

‡ First Discovery of America, p. 46.

§ *Ant. Amer.* p. 36.

name of their own verdant isle, and hence the designation. Exactly when it was discovered is unknown. No records have been preserved of the colony, and its ultimate fate is very uncertain. It has been declared that traces of Irish origin have been found among the native Indian tribes. "In indigenis Americæ Septentrionalis," says Prof. Rafn, "reperiri quædam Hibernicæ originis vestigia, plures docti et experti viri observerunt." * The "vestigia" thus far found, are rather faint, it is true, but there can be no reasonable doubt that a part of America during, and perhaps prior to the tenth century was really settled by the Irish.

We have the account of another supposed discovery of America, about the year 1170. It is related in Lloyd's translation and continuation of Caradoc's History of Wales, published by David Powell in 1584, and is quoted by Hakluyt † in his Book of Voyages. Owen Gwynneth, the prince of northern Wales, died in the year 1170, and his sons fell quarrelling for the possession of the throne. One of these sons, Madoc, becoming disgusted at the conduct of his brothers, threw over his chances for the crown, and taking a vessel sailed out into the open sea, south of Ireland. He sailed west until he came to a strange land, that had apparently never before been visited by Europeans, abounding in many wonderful things. Madoc left most of his people in this new land, and returning to Wales told his countrymen of what he had seen. He invited to accompany him such men and women as preferred a life of peace and quiet to one of turmoil and disturbance at home.

Accordingly a fleet of ten ships left Wales and sailed away to the west, and their crews were never heard of more. There seems no other just inference than that they visited America. Their place of settlement is unknown and has been located all the way from Nova Scotia to Mexico, and from the Atlantic to the Missouri River.

In 1680, more than five centuries after this Welsh emigration, a party of whites were captured by Tuscarora Indians in

* *Antiq. Amer.*, p. 449. † Hawkins *Voyage in Hakluyt Soc.*, p. 111.

South Carolina. One of the captives happening to address another in the Welsh tongue, a Dœg Indian approached him and addressing him in the captives' own language, assured him that he and his friends should not die. To the surprise of the whites it was found that the language of the "Indians" was Welsh. The account was well authenticated, and was preserved in writing by Rev. Morgan Jones,* one of the captives. If really true, it is the most conclusive evidence we have, that Madoc and his fleet did in fact reach America.

John Paul Marana, an Italian, writing about the close of the seventeenth century, concerning an American settlement, says:—"There is a region in that continent inhabited by a people they call Tuscorards and Doegs. Their language is the same as is spoken by the British or Welsh. * * * Those Tuscorards and Doegs of America are thought to be descended from them. * * * 'Tis remarkable also what an Indian king said to a Spaniard, viz.: that in foregoing ages a strange people arrived there by sea, to whom his ancestors gave hospitable entertainment; in regard they found them men of wit and courage, endued also with many other excellencies. * * * The British language is so prevalent here that the very towns, bridges, beasts, birds, rivers, hills, etc., are called by British or Welsh names."† Though these facts would seem to indicate chiefly traces of Madoc's expedition, it has also been suggested‡ that these Welsh-speaking natives might have been descendants of the original settlers of Great Ireland, alluded to above.

Meredith, a Welsh poet, commemorates Madoc's adventures in a Welsh poem, written in 1747. The first four lines of the poem, as translated, are quite sufficient to preclude any desire to see more, being as follows:—

"Madoc I am, the son of Owen Gwynedd,
With stature large and comely grace adorned;
No lands at home, nor store of wealth me please,
My mind was whole to search the western seas."§

---

* See *Gentleman's Magazine*, 1740.

† *Letters writ by a Turkish Spy, etc., written originally in Arabic.* 10th Edition. London, 1734. Vol. viii; p. 159, etc.

‡ Beamish, 216–17.

§ See Belknap's *American Biography*. New York, 1844.

It is said that the histories of the voyage are preserved in the abbeys of Conway and Strat-Flur, and that they furnished materials for other Welsh bards than the one referred to, long before the time of Columbus. Southey, in his long and imaginative poem on this subject, connects the arrival of the Welsh prince with the emigration of the Aztecs, from Aytlan. The Aztecs, under Huitziton, were vanquished by the Welshman and his followers, and were driven from their homes.

> " So in the land
> Madoc was left sole lord; and far away
> Yuhidthiton led forth the Aztecas
> To spread in other lands Mexitli's nam."*

It is unnecessary here to do more than very briefly allude to the remarkable adventures of a celebrated Friesland fisherman, in the fourteenth century. According to his own account, he had crossed the Atlantic and found a wonderful western country called Estotiland. It contained magnificent cities, and its inhabitants were highly civilized, having a language and literature peculiarly their own. In the king's library were some Latin books which no one could read. The fisherman was treated with such exalted attention, that princes fought for possession of him. After an absence of twenty-six years he returned to his own country, and so enthusiastic was his description, that Zichmni, prince of Friesland, in company with a Venetian nobleman named Zeno, determined to see this strange western country. The fisherman, who was to have piloted the expedition, unfortunately died a few days before the intended departure, though this did not prevent the Frieslanders from starting. Zichmni eventually returned to his own country, apparently without having beheld the wonders of Estotiland.† Foster, in his *Northern Voyages*, has implicit faith in the narrative, and argues that Estotiland was nothing else than Vinland, and that the Latin books in the king's library must have once belonged to Eric, the unlucky bishop, who left Greenland in 1121 to convert the descendants of the North-

* Southey's *Madoc*.

† Hakluyt—*Divers Voyages touching the Discovery of America*. London, 1582; p. 72. Pub. for Hakluyt Soc., London.

men, that had degenerated into the idolatry of the native Shraellings.

In Bohun's Geographical Dictionary, published in 1695, Estotiland is described as "a great tract of land in the north of America, toward the Arctic Circle and Hudson's Bay, having New France on the south, and James's Bay on the west, the first of American shores discovered, being found by some Friesland fishers, that were driven hither by a tempest, almost two hundred years before Columbus." Alcedo is more skeptical. According to this writer Estotiland was "an imaginary country which some authors suppose to have been discovered in 1477 by a native of Poland, named John Scalve, and that the same is part of Labrador." The fact is that this island never had any existence, but in the imagination of two brothers of the name of Zanis, Venetian noblemen who had no particular information whatever respecting the expedition of this Polish adventurer; and that in 1497 John Cabot, or Gabot, left England with three of his sons, under the commission of Henry VII, when he discovered Newfoundland, and part of the immediate continent, where this country is supposed to exist. It is a little singular that among the early French and English discoverers a similar rumor existed regarding a powerful city called Norembega, supposed to be situated somewhere in the alleged neighborhood of the imaginary Estotiland. Like Norembega in the north, and the El Dorado at the south, Estotiland must, to use the words of Mr. Belknap, be referred to the fabulous history of America.

Much more trustworthy is the narrative of the Norman sailor, Cousin, a disciple of Descaliers. Infected with the spirit of his age, in the year 1448, Cousin set sail from Dieppe on a voyage of discovery. He sailed southward until, he entered the equatorial current. By this he was drawn westwardly to the South American coast. Landing near the mouth of what is now called the Amazon, he named the river Maragon. Reversing his course he now sailed southeastward, and touched on the southern point of Africa, nearly fifty years before Vasquez de Gama doubled the Cape of Good Hope. Though authentic records of the expedition are no longer extant, the tradition is still preserved among the inhabitants of Dieppe.*

It is said that the mate of Cousin's vessel was named Pinzon, and that he was one of the three brothers of that name who so materially assisted Columbus in his expedition. It is hardly necessary to remind the reader that one of the Pinzons is generally credited with the discovery of Brazil and the Amazon more than half a century after the voyage of the Dieppois sailor. It may be fairly questioned whether greater honor has not been awarded to Pinzon for his supposed discovery than he is entiled to. At all events there is no evidence that he ever disclosed his experience to Columbus.

The only rational conclusion at which we can arrive upon reading these narratives is that America had really been discovered even by Europeans, centuries before Columbus was born. It would be strange indeed if in all the past ages of the world navigators had never been wafted across the ocean. Dim and vague suspicions of the existence of a great "Saturnian continent" beyond the ocean frequently appear in the poetic inspirations of ancient and modern writers long before the time of the Genoese's discoveries. Accounts of western Atlantic discoveries, though of course never matters of general knowledge, were obscurely preserved in the records and literature of the old world. How far Columbus may have been influenced by any knowledge of these discoveries must of course forever remain the subject of conjecture. It is well known that he made a voyage to Iceland in his youth. But whether he had any access to the manuscripts relating to the Vinland colony may well be doubted. His subsequent career and his own theories concerning his discovery would seem to disprove it.

There is a radical distinction, however, between the discoveries by Columbus, and those of his predecessors which we must bear in mind. The latter reached this continent as exiles seeking a new home, as vikings extending their predatory incursions, or as the unwitting sport of the winds and storms.

* See Katharine MacQuoid's "*Through Normandy*," New York, 1875.

The great Admiral started upon his expedition as the representative of the richest kingdom of Europe, with the Spanish throne to sustain him, and with the eyes of the world upon his enterprise. Who can wonder then at the difference in the results? His predecessors came hither as private individuals, whose rulers were too much occupied in fighting their neighbors to care anything about the existence of an uncultivated western continent. Though they came hither in rude and uncivilized ages, yet in the darkest periods they were never guilty of the atrocities committed by the Spaniards with and after Columbus.

ART. II.—1. *The Claims of Labor.* JOHN STEWART MILL. London.
2. *Past and Present.* THOMAS CARLYLE. London.

EDUCATION is the demand one meets with from every quarter—education for the millions. It is pointed to, by the wise doctrinaries of the period, as the north star of civilization, toward which all who would escape from darkness and oppression into a realm of light and liberty must steer their course. The philanthropist and millionaire with their schemes of benevolence and college endowments; the ward politician and would-be statesman; the political reformer and the time-serving place-seeker; in fine, the demagogues and the demi-gods, all find, or profess to find, in the general diffusion of knowledge, and the development of intelligence, a sure specific for all the woes of mankind. One's confidence, well-founded perhaps, in the strength and stability of the American Republic, is in the education of the American people. The general diffusion of the common school system, but lately undertaken in the enlightened centres of Christendom, and the enforcement of the law of "compulsory education," are vainly expected to put wisdom at the helm of state; keep mediocrity out of responsible offices; remove corruption from places of trust; banish pauperism and poor

www.ingramcontent.com/pod-product-compliance
Lightning Source LLC
LaVergne TN
LVHW011132110826
845150LV00008B/2311

* 9 7 8 1 4 1 8 1 9 4 0 4 8 *